BMX
Bikes

by Karol Carstensen

Published By
Capstone Press, Inc.
Mankato, Minnesota USA

Distributed By

𝒸𝒫 CHILDRENS PRESS
CHICAGO

1

CIP
LIBRARY OF CONGRESS CATALOGING IN PUBLICATION DATA

Carstensen, Karol.
  BMX bikes / by Karol Carstensen .
        p. cm. – (Cruisin')
  Summary: Examines BMX bikes, trick riding, racing, and equipment maintenance.

  ISBN 1-56065-076-1:
  1. Bicycle motocross – Juvenile literature. [1. Bicycle motocross. 2. Bicycle racing.] I. Title. II. Series.
  GV1049.3.C37   1989
  796.6'2 – dc20   89-27867
                                                                CIP
                                                                AC

PHOTO CREDITS

Photographs by Jamie Mosberg

CAPSTONE PRESS
Box 669, Mankato, MN 56001

Contents

Pedals Ready...Go!

"There they go, folks! The track is hard and fast. The bumps are wicked and dust is flying everywhere. Number 23 has pulled ahead. He's got a perfect **line** through the first turn..."

BMX is short for bicycle motocross. Boys and girls around the world are enjoying this exciting sport. They are racing and **freestyling** and just having fun.

It all started in the early 1970s. Young riders were inspired by the thrills of motorcycle racing. They began taking their bikes through the jumps, bumps, and turns of the track. They were doing wheelies! Flying high over jumps! Twisting through sharp turns! It was fun and exciting! It was also very hard on the bikes. Bent and twisted wheels and broken frames were common sights.

Bike manufacturers were quick to respond. They began building stronger bikes that could take the hard riding.

In this book you will learn about riding and racing BMX bikes. You will learn how BMX bikes are made and what makes them special. You will also learn how to keep your BMX bike riding smoothly.

Riding The BMX Way

BMX bikes are the most maneuverable bikes ever made. Maneuverable means they are easy to handle. They are small and light. Boys and girls of all ages ride them with ease. BMX bikes are fun to ride. Even a five or six-year old can begin learning to pop wheelies and fly over jumps! BMXers call this **thrashing**.

Most kids get BMX bikes because they want to thrash. They've seen movies with BMXers flying high and doing tricks. Maybe they've seen live demonstrations by BMX daredevils. It looks exciting. It looks fun. It looks radical. Radical, or rad for short, is the BMX word for daring or risky. This kind of BMX riding is called freestyle.

Other BMX owners have their sights set on the race track. They're looking for the challenge of competition. BMX racing is a popular sport. Races are run on dirt tracks. Tracks have turns and jumps to test a rider's skill.

Of course, BMX bikes are also used for everyday riding. They fill the bike racks at schools and playgrounds. They're great for a quick trip to the corner store. They are used to ride around and explore new places. BMX bikes are tough. They can go almost anywhere.

Whether the goal is thrashing, racing, or just riding around, a rider needs to know his or her bike. It is important to get the feel of it. How do the brakes work? Are they hard or easy to operate? How does the bike handle? Does it turn easily? These things show how **responsive** a bike is. A very responsive bike stops quickly and turns corners easily. It does just what the rider wants it to do.

BMX bikes are more responsive than regular street bikes. A new BMX rider needs to get used to this. It only takes a few test rides. Then he or she can go on to learn some basic riding skills and tricks.

Wheelies

A wheelie is when a rider lifts the front wheel and rides on the rear wheel. This is done by lifting up on the handlebars. It takes good balance. With practice, a rider can hold a wheelie for a long time. One expert BMXer set a world record of 4 hours.

Curb Endos

A curb endo is like a reverse wheelie. The rider balances his or her bike on the front wheel. It is done by riding slowly up to a curb. When the front wheel hits the curb, the rider pushes forward on the handlebars. The rear of the bike lifts into the air. Riders try to stay in this position as long as they can. Practicing curb endos helps improve balance. It looks amazing!

Bunny Hops

The bunny hop is a basic jump. It is done on a flat surface without a ramp. At first, riders jump over small objects, like shoeboxes. Shoeboxes are good because they just collapse if you land on them. This is the beginner's first try at taking air. Taking air means jumping to BMXers. In jumping, riders must take off and land on the rear wheel. Landing on the front wheel might send a rider flying over the handlebars! As they get better, riders jump over bigger and bigger objects. The record bunny hop is more than 42 inches long!

Speed Jumps

Racers need to know how to speed jump. It is the fastest way to get over a bump. It is done by pulling a wheelie just when the front wheel hits the top of the bump. The rider sits back over the rear wheel. This keeps the back wheel in the dirt over the top of the bump. Then the front wheel comes down on the other side.

Skids

In a skid, the rear wheel slides out from under the bike on a turn. Practicing skids helps riders get to know their bikes. They want to know how it feels to skid. They want to learn to control skidding on turns. It is a good idea to practice skids on a dirt track or in a field. Skidding too much on concrete will wear out the rear tire.

Cornering

Racers especially need to practice cornering. They want to turn corners fast without skidding. To learn this, they ride through turns faster and faster. They lean their bikes over as far as they can. When the rear wheel starts to slide, they try to keep it straight. Skidding on turns slows a racer down.

Learning these basic skills is fun. Friends practice together. Before long they are popping

wheelies up and down neighborhood streets. They are jumping over everything in sight. Maybe they are ready to try harder tricks.

Freestyle

Freestyle is trick riding. It is the art of total bike control. It was developed by combining the tricks of skateboarding with the BMX bike. Ten years ago, no one knew what freestyle was. Today it is a big part of BMX. There are official freestyle competitions across the United States and in other countries.

Freestylers are cyclists, gymnasts, and stuntmen all rolled into one. They are quick, graceful, and daring. They can make their bikes do just what they want them to do. Freestylers love the challenge of new tricks. They stretch themselves and their bikes to the limit. They are making up new tricks all the time.

Few BMXers can resist trying a few tricks. It is often the reason for getting a BMX bike in the first place. So once in the driver's seat, it's hard not to test it out on bumps and steep hills in the neighborhood. But it takes a lot of practice to learn freestyle tricks. Riders fall many times. Each trick must be mastered before trying the next.

Ramps are used for many tricks. Sometimes a special ramp called a quarterpipe is used. It is shaped like one fourth of a circle. A rider must be very good at bunny hops and speed jumps before trying ramp tricks.

The Cross Up

A cross up is a jump with a little twist. It is done off a ramp or bump. Taking as much air as possible, the rider turns the handlebars to the right or left. The handlebars are turned back before the bike lands.

The Kickout

The kickout is also a jumping trick. It is done by twisting the hips to one side as the bike leaves the ground. This makes the rear of the bike swing out. The front wheel is kept pointing forward.

The Tabletop

A **tabletop** is an extended kickout. It is done by kicking out the bike so far that it is flat on its side in the air. Like a tabletop. This is a very advanced trick. There is also a track obstacle called a tabletop.

The Kickturn

In a kickturn, the rider turns his or her bike around 180 degrees. That is one half of a circle. This is done on a ramp or quarterpipe. Part way up the ramp, the rider lifts the front wheel and leans to the right or left. When the bike is facing back down the ramp, the front wheel comes down. The rider rides away in the same direction he or she came from!

The Aerial

An aerial is like a kickturn in the air. It is done on a quarterpipe. The rider speeds his or her bike up the ramp. At the top, the whole bike is lifted into

the air. Then the rider turns the bike around in mid air. The rear wheel must touch back down on the ramp first.

The Bar Hop

This trick is done on a flat surface. While moving forward at medium speed, the rider lifts his or her knees up to the chin. Then the legs are straightened out over the handlebars. The rider sits on the handlebars and keeps rolling.

The Trackstand

A trackstand is a balancing trick. It is done on a flat surface. The rider balances on a stationary bike. Stationary means the bike is not moving. Trackstands take a lot of control. Riders do handstands and other poses on their bikes.

After these basic freestyle tricks are mastered, riders add their own style to each one. They do one-footers and one-handers. They do can-cans by lifting one leg over the top tube during a crossup. Any new move that comes into a rider's head can become a new trick. But BMXers are always careful. They only try tricks they feel comfortable trying. They always wear safety gear.

Freestyle Competition

Freestylers compete alone or as part of a team.

Riders are divided by age and skill level. They are rated by a panel of experts in the same way that gymnasts or ice skaters are judged. Riders earn points for control and style. Very difficult and original moves help a rider earn more points.

There are flatland and ramp events in freestyle competition. Some riders compete in both, but many specialize. Every competitor must complete certain required moves. Then each rider performs an original routine. The routines are often done to music. Judges look for control and smoothness as well as the difficulty of the moves.

Expert freestyle riders can be chosen to be on a national team. Teams are sponsored by large companies. They travel all over the world to perform. Audiences everywhere love the thrill of watching freestylers do their amazing tricks.

Freestyle Bikes

Freestylers need extra strong bikes. They are thrashing and jumping and crashing all the time. Manufacturers design heavier, stronger frames for freestyle bikes. Stronger **mag wheels** and smooth, high-pressure tires are also used. Most freestyle bikes have two kinds of brakes, coaster brakes and caliper, or hand-operated brakes. Coaster brakes work by pushing backwards on the pedals. Different brakes are used for different tricks.

Some freestyle bikes have special equipment added to them. Framestands, forkstands, and axle pegs attach to different parts of the bike. Riders use them to do more tricks.

Racing

BMX racing is fun for both boys and girls. Racers start as young as 6 years old. Some keep racing until age 16 or older! Racing started when kids got tired of just thrashing around. They wanted to test their riding skills on the racetrack.

The first BMX tracks were built in California in the early 1970s. Before then BMXers raced on the same dirt tracks as motorcycles.

BMX racing quickly gained popularity. By the early 1980s, there were BMX tracks across the United States and in other countries. BMX racing is fun. Racers make lots of new friends. It is good exercise. Best of all, the whole family can get involved. Parents can help out around the track. Brothers and sisters come along to watch and learn.

Today BMX racing is an organized sport. There are local, regional, and national BMX organizations. They see that the racing is fair. They set rules and make sure tracks are good. They also sponsor races.

Any racer can join a national BMX organization. Members pay dues and get racing numbers. The organization keeps track of each member's racing record. Each year, the best racers compete in a national championship. The National Champion's racing number is 1. That is the best prize of all.

Expert racers might be chosen for a national team. Teams are sponsored by bike makers or other big companies. Team members travel to different cities to compete. Sometimes they even go to foreign countries. The sponsor pays all the expenses. The best racers in the country are on the national teams.

Of course, racing doesn't have to be that serious. It's fun to race at a local track. Some towns have tracks that are sponsored by bike shops or service clubs. They have their own championships and prizes. Most kids start out BMX racing this way.

Race Day

The activity of a big track on race day might be surprising to new BMXers. People come from miles around to compete and enjoy the show. Sometimes races last well into the night.

BMX racing is big business. Masses of people come to the track. Food vendors and bike dealers can be seen selling their goods. Hot dogs, pizza, ice cream, T-shirts, stickers, bike gear. It's a full day of fun and excitement for the whole family.

Registration

Racers register when they first get to the track. They need to bring proof of their age. Most bring their birth certificates. The entry fee is $5 to $8. Every racer gets a **number plate**. It is mounted on the handlebars of his or her bike. Racers keep the same number for the whole season. The racing season is from April to October.

Inspection

A race official inspects every racer's bike. He or she makes sure it is safe. Handlebars, frames, and cranks have to be good and tight. Brakes have to work well. Kickstands, fenders, and chainguards must be removed. Bike pads must be in place. The official also makes sure the racer is wearing a helmet and protective clothing. Both the bike and the rider have to pass inspection. If they don't, the rider cannot race that day.

Motos

Soon after registration, the **moto** sheets are posted. A moto is a race. Racers run to the moto board to see which races they are in. The moto sheets sometimes give gate positions too. The racers must know which races they are in. They must be at the starting gate when it's time to race. No one will call their names or come to get them.

Racers are grouped by age and skill level. There are sometimes races just for girls, but boys and girls also race together. Skill levels include beginner, novice, and expert. Every racer starts as a beginner. After winning a certain number of races, he or she moves to the next level. The very best racers can go on to be pros. BMX pros compete for money like professional tennis players and golfers. It takes years of riding to become a BMX pro.

Over 100 motos might be run in one day of racing. There are qualifying motos and a main event. Up to 8 racers compete in each moto. There can be many motos for each age group. Racers who do the best in the motos compete in the main event. There is a main event for each age group and skill level. The best finishers in the main events win trophies.

The Track

BMX races are run on dirt tracks. Tracks can be outdoors or built inside large arenas. The start is set on a small hill. Tracks have turns, bumps, and jumps. There are left and right turns. There are flat turns and banked turns. The banked part of a turn is called the **berm**. There are lots of small bumps that rattle teeth and bones. These are whoop-de-doos, or whoops for short.

There are big jumps with long flat tops that send riders flying. They are called tabletops. There might be a double or triple jump. These are big jumps that are close together. There might also be a drop-off. This is where the track just drops down like a step. But don't worry. There are straight, flat parts, too.

BMX tracks are from 800 to 1400 feet long. A race only lasts a minute. But it is action-packed!

Racers look the track over before the day's action begins. They take a practice ride. They want to know the track. They don't want any surprises in that first moto. They check the dirt. Is it loose or packed? Are there rocks or muddy parts? They check the turns and jumps. Where are they? How sharp are the turns? How big are the jumps? Are there double or triple jumps? What's the best way to get over them fast? Where are the good passing spots? It's important to know the track and have a plan.

The starting gate is also important. A good start helps win a race. Most gates are electronic. They have a **starting light** that counts down the start as is used in drag racing. Racers watch the light and learn its rhythm.

The Race

The racers are lined up, their front wheels close to the gate. All eyes are glued on the starting light. The riders steady their bikes. Red, yellow, green! The gate drops. The racers burst onto the track. The pack is tight. They keep cranking. Tires bite the dirt as the racers near the first turn.

The start is the most important part of a race. Each racer tries to get out of the gate first. A fast start helps put him ahead before the first turn. BMXers call this a **holeshot**. It's good to be ahead early in a race. The leader has an **advantage**. The other racers have to work harder. They have to look for ways to pass.

There are two kinds of starts, one-pedal and two-pedal. Two-pedal starts are best. The racer stands on both pedals. The bike is balanced at the gate ready to go. With one-pedal starts, one foot is on the ground. Time can be lost getting up on the pedals.

Racers try to pedal through the whole race. Sometimes they have to slow down. Sometimes they have to brake. They might put a foot down to avoid a crash. But when they can, they keep cranking the pedals. At first it feels funny to pedal through turns. The inside pedal might dig into the ground. The rear wheel might slide out. It gets easier with practice.

Racers learn how to approach each kind of turn. Banked turns are the fastest. Racers use the berm to speed through them. The pedals have plenty of room to rotate. Sweepers are wide, flat turns. They are fast, too. Pedaling through them is harder, though. Most racers coast through sweepers and pedal when they can. Hairpin turns are very sharp and tricky. Some racers slide around them. They put their foot down for support. The slide must be controlled. A bad slide will cost time in a race.

Turns are a good place to pass other racers. There are many lines, or paths, through a turn. Each racer decides which line he or she will take. The leader tries to block other racers from passing. The second-place rider might swing high up on the berm. Then he or she can gain speed by cutting back toward the inside. This might be enough to shoot past the leader. A racer needs a cool head and quick reactions to find a good line.

BMX races can get rough. Elbows and knees are used to block challengers from passing. Hitting or cutting off another racer is not allowed. Racers who are too rough are disqualified.

Learning to ride the bumps is another racing challenge. Jumping over them is thrilling. The crowd loves it when a racer takes air. But racers can't **accelerate** in the air. High jumps are spectacular. However, in a race, it is wasted time. BMXers say, "Air for show, down for go!"

Of course, there are times when a racer has to jump. The best racers try to stay as low as possible. They want the rear wheel back in the dirt fast.

Double or triple jumps are a real challenge. Some racers take them one at a time. It is safe and it keeps the rear wheel driving hard. Others take to the air and jump two or three at once. It is a daring move that can surprise a competitor who is taking the safe way. It can put a racer ahead, but it is risky. Jumpers are more likely to wipe out.

Good racers keep their eyes ahead at all times. They focus on the track and watch where they are going. Looking at other racers is distracting. Look straight ahead and drive for the finish!

Few racers win when they first start competing. They do the best they can. They set small goals and keep trying. The main goal in BMX racing is to have fun.

BMX Bikes

BMX bikes have to be strong and light. Racers want very light bikes. Lighter bikes can go faster. Most BMX bikes weigh between 20 and 30 pounds. Strength and durability are also important. BMXers are very hard on their bikes.

Bike manufacturers work hard to design strong, light bikes. They make them small and compact. They use strong, light materials like the ones used to build airplanes.

Most BMX bikes are 20-inch bikes. That means they have 20-inch wheels. Regular street bikes have 24-or 26-inch wheels. BMX bikes are smaller and lighter. This makes them fast and easy to steer.

Some BMX bikes have 16-inch wheels. These are for smaller riders and are called minis. Older riders sometimes ride BMX bikes with 26-inch wheels. These bigger bikes are called cruisers. In competition, cruisers race in a separate class.

BMX bikes don't have to be expensive to be good. An expensive bike cannot win the race. The skill of the rider makes the difference. Stock bikes cost from $140 for a starter model to over $600 for a high-tech racer. A stock bike is one that is put together at the factory.

Bike shops sell stock bikes and bike parts. Some riders change parts on their bikes to make them even lighter and stronger. BMXers call this **trickingout** the bike.

Very serious racers sometimes have a special bike just for racing. They choose special parts. They   build their own racing machine. This is very expensive to do. Only sponsored or professional racers can afford it.

A BMX bike has many parts. Each one is designed to withstand hard BMX riding. Most BMXers know all the parts of their bikes. They can read BMX magazines and learn about the newest technology. Bike manufacturers are trying new materials and designs all the time.

The Frame

The bike frame is the most important part of a bike. It is like the foundation of a building. It has to be strong. If the frame is weak, the whole bike will be weak.

The frame is made with three metal tubes. They are the top tube, the down tube, and the seat tube. The three tubes form a triangle, the strongest shape there is. On BMX bikes, the triangle is small so the frames are compact. Compact frames help make BMX bikes small and easy to handle.

Bike frames are made of steel or aluminum. BMX frames are often made of a special steel that is very strong and light. It is called **chrome-moly**.

At the factory, frames are made by welding the three tubes together. Welding is done by melting the ends of two tubes. The melted ends are held together so the metals mix. The hot metal cools and hardens. The tubes stick together and form a joint. Sometimes the walls of the tubes are thicker at the ends. This makes the joints stronger. Metal braces, or gussets, also make the joints stronger.

Welded to the back of the seat tube are two seat stays and two chain stays. Stays are small metal tubes. The seat and chain stays form two rear triangles that hold the rear wheel. They are also made of chrome-moly or another light metal. There are **drop-outs** where the stays come together. This is where the wheel fits. Drop-outs allow the wheel to be adjusted or removed quickly.

The Fork

The front fork is very important on a bike. This

is the part that holds the front wheel. A bike could not be steered without one. The fork also takes most of the shock of hard riding.

Like frames, forks have to be strong and light. They are made of the same material as frames. Forks are thicker than the rear stays. They have to stand up to hard landings, sharp turns and crashes. Forks have drop-outs like the rear stays.

The Handlebars

A rider controls his or her bike with the handlebars. Handlebars have to be strong and secure. They are pushed and pulled in all directions. BMX riders use their handlebars to lift and steer their bikes in amazing ways.

Handlebars are made from a single straight tube. The tube is aluminum or steel. At the factory, the tube is bent to the right shape by a machine. On BMX bikes, a metal bar, or cross brace, is welded between the handle bars. The cross brace adds strength.

Handlebars are connected to the bike by the stem. The stem is a metal clamp. Bolts hold the handlebars securely in the stem. Extra bolts are used to keep BMX handlebars in place. Riding is dangerous if they wobble or slip.

Manufacturers make handlebars of many different shapes and sizes. Shorter riders need lower handlebars. Bigger riders need wider handlebars. Riders choose the ones that fit them best.

The Wheels

The part that the tire fits on is called the wheel. Wheels have to be strong. Whether on a racetrack or in the street, wheels take a lot of punishment. A crash during a race or a fancy trick can bend a wheel. It can be thrown out of alignment. A wheel is aligned when it turns without wobbling or rubbing against any part of the bike.

Almost all BMX bikes have 20-inch wheels. There are two kinds, spoked and mag. Spoked wheels are made of aluminum or steel. Most racers have spoked wheels because they are light. Some wheels have extra spokes to make them stronger. Another kind of wheel is the mag wheel. Mag wheels are molded from a specific plastic. They are heavier than spoked wheels, but stronger. Mag wheels are good for street riding and doing tricks. They last a long time. Mag wheels come in lots of colors.

The Tires

The tires on BMX bikes are called **knobbies**. They are wide and have a deep tread. They are like the tires used on motocross motorcycles but smaller.

Knobbies grip the ground or track. The gripping action is called **traction**. Better traction helps a rider control his or her bike.

The Sprockets

Sprockets are the metal wheels that hold the chain. They have teeth that fit into and drive the chain. BMX bikes are single-speed bikes. They have only one front sprocket and one rear sprocket.

The Cranks

Cranks are the metal pieces that the pedals attach to. Cranks have to be very strong. They help transfer pedal power into rear-wheel power. The rear wheel is what drives the bike forward. Also, cranks take a beating in crashes and skids.

Cranks are made of aluminum or steel. The compact design of BMX frames allow cranks to be long. Longer cranks give more power to each pedal stroke. This is most important at the start of a race. More power means quicker starts.

The Pedals

All BMX bikes have pedals with small teeth on them. They are made of steel or plastic. Pedals are designed to grip the riders' shoes. This keeps their feet from slipping off the pedals. In a race, riders move their feet on and off the pedals many times. One moment they are reaching a foot toward the ground to avoid a crash. The next moment they're back up on the pedals and accelerating fast. Pedals provide a secure place for the riders' feet.

The Brakes

Almost all BMX bikes have caliper brakes. Racers have brakes on the rear wheel only. They do not want the extra weight of front wheel brakes. Also, front wheel brakes can be dangerous at high speeds. A sudden stop could pitch the rider over the handlebars.

Some bikes have coaster brakes. They are useful for doing certain freestyle tricks.

The Seat

Manufacturers make bike seats for every pur-pose. Racers want light, streamlined seats. They choose unpadded racing seats. The seats are not comfortable, but racers don't sit much anyway. Padded seats are better for everyday use.

Bike Maintenance

BMX riders take very good care of their bikes. They check them regularly. If anything needs to be repaired or adjusted, they do it right away. Whether it is used for riding to school or speeding around the track, a bike needs to be kept in good condition. It is unsafe to ride with faulty brakes or loose parts.

Most bicycle maintenance can be done by the owner. All that is needed are a few tools and a little mechanical know-how. There are also experts at most bike shops who can help.

Some of the tools needed for bicycle mainte-nance are wrenches, screwdrivers, and pliers. Many kinds of wrenches are used. There is a special one just for fixing spokes. Extra spokes and materials to fix flat tires are also needed. Some-times parts of a bike need to be lubricated. Oil and grease are used to **lubricate** different parts.

The first task of bicycle maintenance is to pick up the bike and shake it. BMX bikes are light so this is not difficult. If anything rattles or slips, it should be tightened.

Handlebars

Next, the handlebars are checked for play. When they move or slip in the stem, it is called play. To check for play, the rider stands facing the front of the bike. The front wheel is between his or her legs. The bars are pushed and pulled while holding the front wheel steady. They should be secure in the stem. If they slip, the bolts on the stem should be tightened.

Fork

The front fork is also checked for play. A loose fork is tightened by adjusting the parts that attach it to the frame. This is tricky because the fork has ball bearings. Ball bearings are small metal parts that allow things to rotate freely. Wheels and pedals have ball bearings, too.

Wheels

After the handlebars and fork are checked, the bike is turned upside-down. It rests on the seat and handlebars. The wheels are in the air. Spinning the front wheel, the rider looks along the rim. The wheel should be centered in the fork. If needed, it can be adjusted in the drop-out. The front wheel should also spin straight. If it wobbles, the wheel might be bent or the spokes might need adjusting.

Next, the rear wheel is checked in the same way. It can also be adjusted in the drop-out and by tightening spokes.

Spokes

Spokes are checked by plucking each one like a guitar string. They should make a metallic sound. If one sounds flat or dull, it needs to be tightened. A spoke wrench is used to do this. Spokes are tightened a little at a time. After each turn, they are checked again. If spokes are too tight, the wheel can be damaged.

Tires

Tire pressure is checked next. Many riders press on the tire to feel for softness. Others like to be more exact than this. They use a pressure gauge. Tires should be filled to the suggested pressure. Most tires have this information printed on them.

Sometimes racers will use different tire pressures. On hard-packed dirt tracks, softer tires give more traction. If the track is loose dirt, harder tires are used to keep bikes rolling smoothly.

Chains

Bike chains need to be cleaned and oiled. BMX racers and others who ride on dirt a lot do this often. A toothbrush and cleaning solvent will do the trick. Then the chain is oiled again so it turns smoothly. There is a special oil just for chains.

Chain tension is checked by moving the chain up and down. This shows how tight or loose it is. If it is too tight, it will wear out or break. A chain that is too loose will slip off the sprockets. The chain should move up and down about one-half inch. It can be tightened or loosened by moving the rear wheel backward or forward in the drop-out slots.

Cranks

Cranks are checked for play. If needed, they can be tightened. Sometimes the ball bearings get dirty. Dirty ball bearings make a gritty sound when the cranks are turned. Ball bearings can be removed and cleaned. Then they must be greased. There is special grease for ball bearings.

Pedals

Next the pedals are checked. They should be securely attached to the cranks. Also they should spin freely and easily. A little oil will keep pedals working well.

Brakes

Putting the bike upright again, the rider checks the brakes. The space between the brake shoes and the wheel should be the same on both sides. Brake shoes are the rubber pieces that squeeze the wheel and make the bike stop. They should be close to the wheel, but not touching it. Closer brake shoes make the brakes more responsive. Responsive brakes work quickly and easily. This helps riders control their bikes better.

Sometimes brakes loosen up and stopping is difficult. This means the brake cable is stretched. The cable goes from the brake lever on the handlebars to the brake assembly on the wheel. It can be easily tightened.

Coaster brakes are harder to adjust. Most owners get them fixed at the repair shop.

Frame

Last, it is a good idea to check the bike frame before riding again. If there are cracks or weak spots, they should be repaired at the shop. Bike pads should be in place and secure. A fine-tuned machine is important, and so is safety.

Safety

BMX bikes are built for the thrills of hard riding. Riders certainly get the most out of them. Fearless tricks and fierce competitions make our hearts beat fast. But fearless tricks are learned after many tries. Crashes on the racetrack are common. Falling is a part of BMX riding. But riders hardly ever get seriously hurt. In fact, BMX is safer than sports like football or soccer.

Riders do a lot to reduce the risk of injury. First, they always wear helmets. In fact, all bikers should wear helmets. It is a requirement in BMX competition.

There are two kinds of helmets, full-face and open-face. Full-face helmets cover the head, cheeks, chin, and mouth. They protect the face and teeth. Open-face helmets just cover the head. A separate **mouthguard** is worn with open-face helmets.

Helmets are kept on with a chin strap. They should fit securely. The chin strap should be fastened at all times when riding. A helmet is useless if it flies off on the first jump.

Helmets are made of strong fiberglass. They have a padded liner that fits snugly and adds protection.

It is also a good idea to have a visor. The visor is attached to the front of the helmet. It blocks the sun from the rider's eyes.

Helmets come in many colors and styles. Custom-painted helmets are popular. These are one-of-a-kind helmets painted especially for one person. A good helmet costs about $70. It is worth it to get the best. It is the most important protection a rider wears.

Most BMX racers wear goggles, too. Racers kick up a lot of dirt on the track. Goggles help them see and also protect the eyes from injury.

Riders wear protective clothing as well. Long-sleeved shirts and long pants help guard against skinned elbows and knees. In competition, elbow pads are required when riders are wearing short-sleeved shirts. Most racers also wear knee pads. Pads are worn under clothing so they are out of the way. Bruises and scrapes are a part of any BMXers life. Proper clothing helps BMX riders protect against more serious injury.

BMXers can buy special padded pants called leathers. Leathers are made of strong synthetic, or man-made material. They have padded hips, knees, and shins. They have tight legs, too. BMX racing bikes do not have chainguards. Loose fitting pants can get caught in the chain and cause disaster. Racers sometimes get jerseys to match their leathers. BMX jerseys have built-in elbow pads.

Any soft-sole shoes that the pedals can grip are good for riding. Most BMXers wear canvas shoes. Lace-up shoes stay on better than slip-ons. Hightops help protect ankles from cuts and scrapes. Canvas BMX shoes come in many styles, colors, and patterns. Many riders just wear basketball or running shoes.

Special bicycle gloves are worn to protect hands from cuts and scrapes. They have rubber strips or bumps on the palms to help riders grip the handlebars.

Clothes and pads do a lot to protect riders. For added safety, BMXers also pad their bikes. Falling onto the top tube or flying into the handlebar is no fun. Bike pads help soften the blow. Manufacturers make special safety pads for the top tube, the cross brace, and the stem of BMX bikes. Pads come in many slick racing colors.

Fully protected, BMXers can go out and do some really radical riding!

To Learn More

There are many ways to learn more about BMX bikes and competition. Your local bike shop is a good place to start. Bike dealers are very friendly and helpful. Also, you can get books and magazines at the library. Two good magazines are BMX ACTION and BMX PLUS.

For further information, contact the organization listed below.

American Bicycle Association
P.O. Box 718
Chandler, AZ 85224

Glossary

Accelerate
To increase speed.

Advantage
To be in a better position than another.

Berm
The bank of a turn. When used tactically in a race, it is called berm warfare.

Bike Pads
Foam pads put on a bike to protect the rider from injury.

Chrome-moly
A mixture of steels that is very strong and light. It is used to make many bike parts.

Drop-out
A slot at the bottom of the fork and stays into which the axle of a wheel fits.

Freestyle
Trick riding on a BMX bike. Also the branch of BMX in which riders display tricks and riding skills.

Holeshot
Moving into the lead before the first turn in a race.

Knobbies
Special deep-tread racing tires made for BMX bikes.

Line
A fast and strategic path on a race track.

Lubricate
To make slippery.

Mag Wheels
Strong durable plastic wheels.

Moto
A qualifying race.

Mouthguard
Protective covering for mouth and chin worn in BMX racing.

Number Plate
Plastic piece mounted on handlebars to hold racing number.

Responsive
Quick to react.

Starting Light
Electronic device used to start a race. Looks like a stoplight with two yellow lights.

Tabletop
A freestyle trick in which the rider turns the bike onto its side in mid-air. Also a flat-topped jump on a race track.

Taking Air
Jumping on a bike so that both wheels come off the ground.

Thrashing
Doing bike tricks for fun.

Traction
Friction between the tire and the ground allowing the tire to get hold of the track.

Trickingout
Changing parts on a bike to make it more race-worthy.